A CHRISTMAS CAROL

A One-Act Dramatisation

By Constance Cox

From the story by Charles Dickens

samuelfrench.co.uk

Copyright © 1968 Constance Cox
All Rights Reserved

A CHRISTMAS CAROL is fully protected under the copyright laws of the British Commonwealth, including Canada, the United States of America, and all other countries of the Copyright Union. All rights, including professional and amateur stage productions, recitation, lecturing, public reading, motion picture, radio broadcasting, television and the rights of translation into foreign languages are strictly reserved.

ISBN 978-0-573-11690-2

www.samuelfrench.co.uk
www.samuelfrench.com

FOR AMATEUR PRODUCTION ENQUIRIES

UNITED KINGDOM AND WORLD
EXCLUDING NORTH AMERICA
plays@samuelfrench.co.uk
020 7255 4302/01

Each title is subject to availability from Samuel French,
depending upon country of performance.

CAUTION: Professional and amateur producers are hereby warned that *A CHRISTMAS CAROL* is subject to a licensing fee. Publication of this play does not imply availability for performance. Both amateurs and professionals considering a production are strongly advised to apply to the appropriate agent before starting rehearsals, advertising, or booking a theatre. A licensing fee must be paid whether the title is presented for charity or gain and whether or not admission is charged.

The Professional Rights in this play are controlled by Samuel French Ltd (A Concord Theatricals Company), Aldwych House, 71-91 Aldwych, London, WC2B 4HN.

No one shall make any changes in this title for the purpose of production. No part of this book may be reproduced, stored in a retrieval system, or transmitted in any form, by any means, now known or yet to be invented, including mechanical, electronic, photocopying, recording, videotaping, or otherwise, without the prior written permission of the publisher. No one shall upload this title, or part of this title, to any social media websites.

The right of Constance Cox to be identified as author of this work has been asserted in accordance with Section 77 of the Copyright, Designs and Patents Act 1988.

© Constance Cox   1968

CHARACTERS

SCROOGE	MR. FEZZIWIG
BOB CRATCHIT	MRS. FEZZIWIG
SCROOGE'S NIECE	MRS. CRATCHIT
1st LADY	MARTHA CRATCHIT
2nd LADY	TOM CRATCHIT
MARLEY'S GHOST	PAWNBROKER
THE SPIRIT OF CHRISTMAS	LAUNDRESS
YOUNG SCROOGE	CHARWOMAN
FANNY	Guests at Fezziwig's party

Winner of the Myra Stewart Cup for the Best Costume Play presented in the 1967 Drama Festival of the Sussex Federation of Townswomens' Guilds.

The scene throughout is Scrooge's office on Christmas Eve and Christmas Day. Period 1840.

There is an acting fee of twenty-five shillings on each and every performance of 'A CHRISTMAS CAROL'. The fee is payable to Evans Brothers Limited, Montague House, Russell Square, London W.C.1. or any of their authorised agents overseas, who will then issue a licence giving permission for the performance to take place. A licence MUST be issued before any representation may take place. The fee cannot in any circumstances be varied or waived.

AGENTS

from whom copies and licences may be obtained

AUSTRALIA	Will Andrade, 173 Pitt Street, Sydney.
NEW ZEALAND	The Play Bureau, Box 3611, Wellington.
SOUTH AFRICA	Rene Ahrenson, Eirene, Gibson Road, Kenilworth, Cape Town.
KENYA, UGANDA and TANZANIA	Master Play Agencies, Kenya National Theatre, P.O. Box 452, Nairobi.

Printed in Great Britain by offset lithography by
Billing & Sons Limited, Guildford and London

237 49495 7   PR. 4611

A CHRISTMAS CAROL

The scene is SCROOGE'S office.   Late afternoon - winter.

Light is fading in the office which is shabbily and sparsely furnished with only the barest of necessities.   SCROOGE'S desk is angled at R. of the stage, and CRATCHIT'S is similarly placed at L. opposite to his employer's. On each desk there is a lighted candle, an inkstand, and pens, various documents and ledgers.   Against the centre of the back wall is a cupboard with shelves above it on which are law books, files, an odd deed box, and more papers.   On either side of this cupboard are two wooden chairs.   A large hat-stand is U.R. and on it hang the hats and coats of the two occupants of the office.   A fire burns down in the footlights C. with fender and fire-irons, and in front of the fire is placed a stool.   Chairs for SCROOGE and CRATCHIT are behind their desks.

As the curtain rises SCROOGE and BOB CRATCHIT are seated at their desks.   SCROOGE is writing in a ledger.   BOB is surreptitiously warming his hands at his candle.   Outside the sound of voices can be heard singing "God Rest Ye Merry, Gentlemen".   BOB smiles in appreciation, rises and moves to cupboard C, where he opens a law book, checks a reference, and returns to his desk to stand at top corner.   SCROOGE looks up.

SCROOGE	What's that?
BOB	What's what, sir? (Making an entry in ledger.)
SCROOGE	That screeching - that caterwauling going on outside.
BOB	It's the waits, sir. (Moves and sits at his desk.)
SCROOGE	Waits? What are the waits doing in this corner of London?

A CHRISTMAS CAROL

BOB (smiling nervously) It's the custom, sir, at Christmas, to visit even the business quarters.

SCROOGE Custom? What have we to do with custom, except the kind that brings in money! Tell 'em to move on, Cratchit. Well, go on!

BOB (rising reluctantly) It's good of them, sir, to have taken so much trouble to try and entertain us. It's freezing outside. (Moves C.)

SCROOGE (rising) Tell 'em I'll warm 'em with this ruler – (Snatches it up, and moves to top of desk.) if they don't move on! They don't entertain me – nor did I ask them to come.

(Voices stop, and there is a knocking on the door.)

And if that's them asking for money – well, see who it is! Go on! What do you think I pay you for?

BOB (moving to U.L.) I was just going, sir. (He goes off U.L. and returns almost immediately.) Why, sir, it's Mrs. Fred! (Moves C.)

(SCROOGE'S NIECE, a young pretty woman, enters.)

NIECE (coming to BOB'S L.) A merry Christmas to you, Mr. Cratchit.

BOB And a merry Christmas to you, ma'am.

NIECE (crossing BOB to SCROOGE'S desk) A merry Christmas, uncle.

SCROOGE Bah! Humbug!

(BOB brings a chair for her from R. of cupboard, and places it in front of the desk.)

NIECE Christmas a humbug, uncle? You don't mean that, I'm sure. (She sits, smiling her thanks to BOB who stands on her L.)

SCROOGE I do mean it. Merry Christmas, indeed! What right have you to be merry? You're poor enough.

NIECE (smiling) Well, then, uncle, what right have you to be dismal? You're rich enough.

A CHRISTMAS CAROL

(BOB laughs.)

SCROOGE — Another sound from you, Cratchit, and you'll be looking for a situation. That'll give you something to be merry about.

(BOB hastily returns to his desk and sits, resuming his work.)

Now, niece, state your purpose here. I'm busy.

NIECE — Don't be angry, uncle. I came to ask you to dine with us tomorrow.

SCROOGE — Dine with you? I'll see you and your husband at the devil first.

NIECE — But why? Why?

SCROOGE — Why did you get married?

NIECE — (smiling) Because I fell in love.

SCROOGE — (disgusted) Because you fell in love! Humbug! (Takes up pen.) Good afternoon.

NIECE — But, uncle, you never came to see me before that happened. Why give it as a reason for not coming now?

SCROOGE — (writing) Good afternoon.

NIECE — I want nothing from you. I ask nothing from you. Why can't we be friends?

SCROOGE — Good afternoon.

NIECE — (rising) Well, remember, if you should change your mind, we shall be so glad to see you. (She holds out her hand. SCROOGE ignores it.) Goodbye, uncle.

(There is no movement from SCROOGE. She sighs and moves up C. BOB rises quickly and moves up to her L.)

BOB — Let me see you down the path, ma'am. It's slippery.

NIECE — How are your family, Mr. Cratchit?

BOB — Oh, bobbish, thank you, ma'am. Pretty bobbish. Looking forward to tomorrow, ma'am.

(NIECE crosses him to move U.L. He follows talking.)

Oh, we shall make merry, you know, in our own small way –

(They have gone out U.L. SCROOGE rises, and moves

A CHRISTMAS CAROL

	round the bottom of his desk to fire, looking after them.)
SCROOGE	There's another idiot, my clerk. A fellow with fifteen shillings a week talking about a merry Christmas! They're all mad! (Moves back to bottom of desk.) Everybody's mad but me, or I'll retire to Bedlam!
	(BOB returns.)
	Oh, you've come back to work, have you?
BOB	(moving C.) If you please, sir, there's two more ladies asking to see you, sir.
	(Two ladies enter U.L. The 2nd LADY carries a small note book. BOB turns to them as they hesitate U.L.)
	(To 1st LADY; indicating SCROOGE) That's the principal of the firm, ma'am.
1st LADY	Thank you. (Crosses to front of SCROOGE'S desk; followed by 2nd LADY.) This is Scrooge and Marley, I believe?
	(SCROOGE inclines his head.)
	Have I the pleasure of addressing Mr. Scrooge or Mr. Marley?
SCROOGE	Mr. Marley has been dead these seven years. He died seven years ago this very night. (To BOB, who is watching.) Cratchit!
BOB	(hastily) Yes, sir. (He returns to his desk, sits and resumes work.)
	(SCROOGE moves and sits behind his desk.)
1st LADY	Then I have no doubt that his liberality is well represented in his surviving partner. (She sits in the chair by the desk.) At this season of the year, Mr. Scrooge, it is more than usually desirable that we should make some slight provision for the poor and destitute. Many thousands suffer greatly at the present time, sir. Hundreds of thousands are in want of common comforts.
SCROOGE	Are there no prisons?
1st LADY	(slightly startled) Plenty of prisons.
SCROOGE	And the workhouses? Are they still in operation?

1st LADY	They are.
2nd LADY	I wish we could say they were not.
1st LADY	But under the impression, sir, that they scarcely furnish Christian cheer of mind and body to the multitude, a few of us are endeavouring to raise a fund to buy the poor some meat and drink and means of warmth. (She takes a notebook from the 2nd LADY.) Now, Mr. Scrooge, what shall I put you down for?
SCROOGE	Nothing.
1st LADY	You wish to remain anonymous?
SCROOGE	(violently) I wish to be left alone! I don't make merry myself at Christmas, and I can't afford to make idle people merry! I help to support the establishments I mentioned, and those are who badly off must go there!
1st LADY	Many can't go there, sir!
2nd LADY	And many would rather die!
SCROOGE	(rising) If they'd rather die they'd better do it and decrease the surplus population! You waste my time, ma'am, and time is money to me.
	(1st LADY rises.)
	Cratchit, show these ladies out! (Sits.)
BOB	(rising quickly, moving up to C.) Yes, sir.
	(The 2nd LADY crosses BOB and goes off. The 1st LADY remains a second to stare indignantly at SCROOGE, then turns and crosses BOB to U.L. As she passes him, BOB detains her.)
	(Softly.) Excuse me, ma'am. (Feels in pocket.) If I might - (Gives a coin.) just a trifle.
1st LADY	(warmly) Thank you, sir. Thank you, indeed. A merry Christmas to you. (Turns to go.)
BOB	(following her to U.L.) And to you, ma'am.
	(As the 1st LADY goes, a clock offstage begins to strike five. BOB moves to C, looking at SCROOGE expectantly.)

A CHRISTMAS CAROL

Er – it's five o'clock, sir.

SCROOGE I heard it. All right, be off with you.

BOB Thank you, sir. (He replaces chair from front of SCROOGE'S desk to its place R. of cupboard, then moves to his own desk, closes his ledger, and takes it up to place on shelf above cupboard.)

SCROOGE (rising, coming to bottom of the desk, speaking as BOB goes up C. with ledger) You'll want all day tomorrow, I suppose?

BOB If quite convenient, sir. (Takes muffler and hat from hat-stand.)

SCROOGE (moving to front of desk) It's not convenient, and it's not fair.

(BOB comes down to SCROOGE'S L.)

If I was to stop half a crown for it, you'd think yourself ill-used, I'll be bound. Yet you don't think me ill-used when I pay a day's wages for no work.

BOB It's only once a year, sir.

SCROOGE A poor excuse for picking a man's pocket every twenty-fifth of December. But I suppose you must have the whole day, (Breaks to bottom of desk.) Be here all the earlier next morning.

BOB (delighted) Yes, sir. I will, sir. Goodnight, sir – goodnight and a merry – er – goodnight, sir.

(He goes off U.L. SCROOGE glares after him.)

SCROOGE Fools, fools, the lot of them! (He sees the lighted candle on BOB'S desk.) Wasteful, too! (Crosses and blows it out.) My word, but it's cold tonight. (Moves to fire.) I'll take my supper down here while there's a bit of fire left. It's a pity to waste it. (Sits on stool. He takes bellows from beside the fire and blows on the coals. The wind rises, moaning fitfully about the house.) Strange – there's a face in the fire. Yes, a face as plain as plain. It's like Marley's face – Marley's – Why should I think of Marley now? Marley's been dead these seven years. Humbug! (He takes the poker to destroy the image, when a clanking noise is heard off. He puts the poker down.) What's that?

A CHRISTMAS CAROL

(Rises, and moves U.C., looking towards U.L.)   Who's there? We're closed – the door is locked.   You can't come in!

(The ghost of MARLEY enters U.L.   He is heavily fettered with a long chain on which are hung keys, purses, cash-boxes and a small cash book or two.   The GHOST moves slowly to C. then stops.   SCROOGE backs away.)

MARLEY Neither locks nor bolts can stay me, Ebenezer.

SCROOGE What do you want?   Who are you?

MARLEY Ask me rather who I was.   In life I was your partner, Jacob Marley.

SCROOGE Marley! No – no – it's indigestion.   (Moves down R. to bottom of desk.)   I won't believe it!

MARLEY You don't believe in me?

SCROOGE (turning)   No, I don't.

MARLEY Yet you saw my face in the coals just now, as a warning I was coming.   I have sat invisible beside you many and many a day.

SCROOGE (moving slowly R.)   Are you a ghost, Jacob?

MARLEY I am a ghost, and I am come to warn you.   Do you see this chain I bear?

SCROOGE I do, Jacob.   It's a heavy chain indeed.

MARLEY It is the chain I forged myself in life.   I made it link by link and yard by yard.   Is its pattern strange to you?

SCROOGE No.   (He moves round above MARLEY as he speaks, ending by top end of desk L.)   I see cash boxes – purses – keys – padlocks – ledgers.   Why are you fettered with these, Jacob?

MARLEY I wear the things I worshipped in my life – as you will wear them, Ebenezer, in your death.   Only your chain will be four times as heavy and as long as this.

SCROOGE You said you came to warn me, Jacob.   What is it you'd warn me of?

MARLEY How to escape the fate that I am doomed to.   Listen to me,

A CHRISTMAS CAROL

        Ebenezer. You have still a hope - a hope and chance of my procuring.

SCROOGE   You were always a good friend to me, Jacob. Thank 'ee.

MARLEY   You will be haunted, Ebenezer, by a spirit.

SCROOGE   (backing to D.L.) A spirit! It's - it's very kind of you, Jacob, but I think I'd rather not.

MARLEY   Without her help you cannot hope to shun the path I tread. (He moves towards U.L.) Expect her when the clock strikes next.

SCROOGE   (moving to U.C. level with him) Jacob -

MARLEY   (turning in doorway) For your own sake, Ebenezer, remember what has passed between us.

        (The lights fade down. The wind howls. MARLEY fades into the darkness U.L.)

SCROOGE   (swallowing) Humbug! That's what it is, humbug! (Crosses to desk R., takes his candle from it, crosses to desk L., and lights the other candle from it. The lights come up a little.) He was never there. I only thought I saw him. It's my liver for certain. An undigested bit of beef - a crumb of cheese - a lump of underdone potato, and a man may see anything. (Holding a candle still in his hand, he feels for his watch.) What time is it? (Takes out watch.) On the half hour now, and there's nothing.

        (A clock offstage booms once. The candle goes out in SCROOGE'S hand. SCROOGE gasps, and turns, feeling a presence. THE SPIRIT OF CHRISTMAS stands U.R.).

        Are - are you the spirit whose coming was foretold to me? (Backs against desk, putting candle on it.)

SPIRIT   (coming C) I am. (Her manner is compassionate, and her voice benign and gentle.)

SCROOGE   Who and what are you?

SPIRIT   The Spirit of Christmas Past.

SCROOGE   Christmas past? Long past?

SPIRIT	No - your past. (She stretches out her arm.) Touch my hand.
	(SCROOGE hesitates.)
	Touch my hand.
	(SCROOGE moves and touches her hand. As she speaks again, he backs against desk R.)
	Now look. What do you see? (Backs to top of desk R.)
	(The lights come up much higher than before. SCROOGE looks about him in amazement.)
SCROOGE	Why - it's my old classroom - at the school I attended as a boy!
	(YOUNG SCROOGE enters, reading. He comes D.C. and sits on the stool before the fire.)
	Why have you brought me back here?
SPIRIT	So that you might remember all you have forgotten. Do you see who is reading there?
	(SCROOGE moves to L. of stool as he speaks, looking at YOUNG SCROOGE.)
SCROOGE	Yes - myself. All had gone home for the holidays but me. I had no place to go. (Crossing behind stool to D.R.) No one but my books.
SPIRIT	No one?
	(A GIRL'S voice calls off.)
FANNY	(off) Ebenezer! Ebenezer, where are you?
Y. SCROOGE	(mystified) Fan?
	(FANNY runs in. She is a young girl of the age of SCROOGE'S NIECE, with whom the part can be doubled.)
FANNY	(holding out her arms) Oh, dear brother!
	(YOUNG SCROOGE rises and moves up to her. They embrace.)
	Dear, dear brother!
Y. SCROOGE	(overjoyed) Fan!

A CHRISTMAS CAROL

FANNY (laughing and kissing him) Yes!

Y. SCROOGE Why, what are you doing here?

FANNY I've come to bring you home, dear brother! To bring you home - home - home!

Y. SCROOGE (crossing her to desk L., the happiness fading from his face) Home, Fan?

FANNY (coming behind him, her hands on his arms) Yes, for good and all - for ever and ever! Father's so much kinder than he used to be, that home's like heaven! And you're to be a man now and never come back here.

Y. SCROOGE (turning to her, delighted) Never come back? Oh, Fan!

FANNY (taking his hands) But first we're all to be together all the Christmas long, and have the merriest time in all the world at Mr. Fezziwig's!

Y. SCROOGE But why should Mr. Fezziwig invite us?

FANNY He has a situation ready for you, Ebenezer! Oh, he's so good and kind! Come, get your box. The coach is waiting for us!

Y. SCROOGE (picking up the book he has dropped by the fire) Oh, Fan, we'll have such a Christmas!

FANNY (taking his hand and pulling him U.L.) Such a merry, merry Christmas!

(They go off together laughing. SCROOGE crosses to U.L. looking after them.)

SCROOGE And such a merry Christmas it was, too. The first of many. When I think of all the eating and drinking - and the music and the dancing that went on -.

(Music of "Sir Roger de Coverley" sounds offstage.)

I swear I hear the music of that dancing now! (Moves to below desk L.)

SPIRIT You do. Behold!

(Enter from U.L. MR. FEZZIWIG, a merry old gentleman, MRS. FEZZIWIG, a plump old lady. Several guests follow,

A CHRISTMAS CAROL   11

                    including YOUNG SCROOGE and FANNY, who has now
                    taken off bonnet and cloak. They are laughing with one
                    another.)

SCROOGE   Why, it's Fezziwig himself, bless his heart! It's Fezziwig
                    alive again!)

FEZZIWIG   Now then, everybody, take your partners. Mrs. Fezziwig,
                    do me the honour!

MRS. F.   With pleasure, Mr. Fezziwig.

                    (They form two lines and dance "Sir Roger de Coverley".
                    Then as the music ends:)

FEZZIWIG   Now, everybody, to the food! There's turkey and ham,
                    roast beef and the punch bowl - all hot and just asking for your
                    attention! Away with you now!

                    (The GUESTS and MRS. FEZZIWIG go off U.L., laughing
                    and talking. YOUNG SCROOGE is about to follow when
                    FEZZIWIG detains him, standing C, with YOUNG SCROOGE
                    on his left.)

FEZZIWIG   Ebenezer, a word with you.

Y. SCROOGE   Sir?

FEZZIWIG   Ebenezer, do you know what year it is?

Y. SCROOGE   That I do, sir. Eighteen hundred and one.

FEZZIWIG   And something more. The year that you come out of your
                    apprenticeship to me. You see that desk there, Ebenezer -
                    (He indicates desk L.)   - that one placed near my own?
                    That will be your desk in future.

Y. SCROOGE   Mine?   (He moves to it and touches it.)   But - it's
                    your head clerk's desk, sir.   (Turning.)

FEZZIWIG   (smiling)   Yes.

Y. SCROOGE   Sir - am I to be -?   (Moves to him.)   Mr. Fezziwig,
                    do you really mean it?

FEZZIWIG   (laying a hand on his shoulder)   I really mean it, Ebenezer.
                    You have earned it. Work well, and don't betray my trust.
                    (He puts his arm about YOUNG SCROOGE'S shoulders.)
                    Now let us go to supper. It's Christmas and a time for us all
                    to be merry.

12 A CHRISTMAS CAROL

(FEZZIWIG and YOUNG SCROOGE go off U.L. SCROOGE buries his face in his hands, then crosses and sits on the stool before the fire. Lights fade to candlelight.)

SPIRIT (moving down to stand on his R.)   Did you betray his trust?

SCROOGE (miserably)   Oh, Spirit, you know everything! Why ask me that? I turned the chance he gave me to my own advantage. I brought him to ruin — and he had been so good to me.

SPIRIT Good? How?

SCROOGE How? You saw the joy he brought to everyone!

SPIRIT He spent a few pounds of your mortal money — three or four, perhaps. Is that so much that he deserves this praise?

SCROOGE (indignantly)   It wasn't that! He had the power to make us happy or unhappy — to make our service light or burdensome — a pleasure or a toil. The happiness he gave was quite as great as if it cost a fortune. Oh, Spirit!

SPIRIT What is it?

SCROOGE (rising; moving to desk L.)   Nothing. Only I should like to be able to say a word to my clerk just now, that's all.

(THE SPIRIT stretches out her arm. SCROOGE crosses to her, afraid.)

Spirit, show me no more! Be merciful! Why do you delight to torture me?

SPIRIT (backing to U.R.)   Look and learn.

(The lights come up to full. SCROOGE backs to D.R. as voices are heard. MRS. CRATCHIT, a plump motherly woman, enters U.L. carrying a tray on which are two glasses and two cups. MARTHA CRATCHIT, a girl in the twenties, follows, holding a bottle from which she is taking the cork.)

MRS. C. Where has your precious father got to, and your brother Tom? (Puts tray on desk L.)   They weren't as late as this last Christmas Day by half an hour.

MARTHA Never mind, mother, the dinner won't spoil.

MRS. C. That it won't. I'll see to that. Give me that bottle, Martha,

A CHRISTMAS CAROL   13

and put the chairs before the fire.

(MARTHA moves upstage to chair L. of cupboard, as BOB CRATCHIT and TOM CRATCHIT enter U.L. wearing hats and mufflers.   TOM is about fourteen.)

MARTHA Here's father!   Dear father!   (Embraces him.)   Merry Christmas!

BOB Merry Christmas to you, Martha, my dear.   It's good to have you home.

(MRS. CRATCHIT meanwhile has taken off TOM'S hat and muffler and put them on the desk.   MARTHA brings up L. chair to L. of fire.   TOM crosses and brings down U.R. chair to R. of fire, turns it and straddles it, stretching hands to the fire.   MARTHA sits on the stool.)

MRS. C. (to BOB)   Sit you down before the fire, my dear, and have a warm and a drink, Lord bless you, before we have dinner.

BOB Dinner, eh?   (Rubbing his hands and sitting on chair L. of fire.)   I must say I'm ready for it.

TOM Oh, father, there's such a goose!   You never saw such a goose!

BOB (laughing, and chucking MARTHA under the chin)   Except for this one here, eh, Martha, my dear?

MARTHA (laughing)   Father!

(MRS. CRATCHIT is filling cups and glasses from the bottle at desk L.)

BOB It's not quite so big, but big as big can be!   Oh, mother, show it to him, please!

MRS. C. Your father will see it soon enough, when I bring it to the table.

TOM Oh, mother, please!   It looks so beautiful!

MRS. C. Oh, very well.   But have your drinks first.   (Hands glass to BOB and cup to MARTHA.   Then picks up other cup.)   And there's a little drop for Tom as well - (She crosses to him with the cup.)   - seeing as it's only elderberry wine.   (She ruffles his hair affectionately,

A CHRISTMAS CAROL

then goes off U.L.)

BOB   What else is there for dinner, Tom, besides the goose?

TOM   (excited)   Oh, father, there's mashed potatoes –

BOB   Splendid!

TOM   And apple sauce and sage and onion!

BOB   Better and better!

TOM   And gravy! Oh, and, father, there's a pudden!

BOB   (with mock astonishment)   Not a Christmas pudding, Tom? You don't mean there's a Christmas pudding?

TOM   (nodding vigorously)   It's boiling in the copper now! It's big and round – it's like a great cannon ball!

BOB   Well, bless my soul, we've got a dinner fit for any king.

(MRS. CRATCHIT enters U.L. bearing on a large plate the smallest goose you ever saw.)

MARTHA   And here's the goose! Look, father!

(They rise fascinated and crowd around MRS. CRATCHIT.)

TOM   Isn't it a splendid goose, father?

BOB   My, my, my, I never saw such a bird! We must drink a toast to it.

(MRS. CRATCHIT places the plate on the stool. BOB takes glass from desk. TOM withdraws to R. of fire where every now and then he tries to touch the goose. MARTHA stands C. behind fire. MRS. CRATCHIT stands on BOB'S R.)

Come, here's your glass, my dear. And now I give you Mr. Scrooge, the founder of the feast.

MRS. C.   (her smile fading; with asperity)   The founder of the feast indeed! I wish I had him here. I'd give him a piece of my mind to feast upon, and I hope he'd have a good appetite for it.

BOB   My dear, it's Christmas Day.

MRS. C.   And he's an odious, stingy, hard, unfeeling man. (Gently.) You know he is, Robert. Nobody knows it better than you do.

BOB	We should forget these things, my dear, on Christmas Day. Come now.
MRS. C.	(giving in) I'll drink his health for your sake and the day's - but not for his. (Raises her glass.) A long life and a merry Christmas and a happy New Year to him. And happy, and very merry he'll be, I've no doubt.
BOB	Mr. Scrooge!
MARTHA) TOM)	Mr. Scrooge!
BOB	(taking her glass) And now for the dinner! (Puts his own and his wife's glass on tray and picks it up.) Bring along that magnificent bird, my dear.
	(MRS. CRATCHIT picks up the plate and leads the way off.)
	Come, Martha, come, Tom. The feast is ready!
	(MRS. CRATCHIT bears out the goose holding it high. BOB, MARTHA and TOM follow singing "Good King Wenceslas" and beating time on their cups with their fingers. They all go off U.L. SCROOGE moves to U.C. looking after them. He turns to the SPIRIT. The lights fade to candlelight.)
SCROOGE	Spirit, is that all the dinner they have? For that family?
SPIRIT	(crossing to D.L.) Love and thankfulness will sit at their table. They will think it a banquet. (She stretches out her arm, and beckons him to stand by her.)
SCROOGE	(moving to front of desk L.) Must I see more yet?
SPIRIT	But one more Christmas. A Christmas yet to come.
	(She raises her arms. The lights come up. A dirty-looking MAN in spectacles and taking snuff, enters U.L. and crosses to behind desk R.)
SCROOGE	Who's that man? I don't know him.
	(A LAUNDRESS and a CHARWOMAN enter U.L. Both are carrying bundles.)
SPIRIT	But you know these women, I believe.

SCROOGE	My laundress and my charwoman! What is this place?
BROKER	Now then ladies, bundles forward! Who'll be the first?
LAUNDRESS	Let the charwoman be first. I don't mind waiting. The things I've got won't fly away.
CHARWOMAN	(crossing to front of desk R.) Here you are then, Joe. (Puts bundle on the counter.) Let me know the wally(value) of it.)
	(THE LAUNDRESS sits on stool, facing up towards desk R.)
BROKER	Not very heavy, Mrs. Diller. (Unties it.)
CHARWOMAN	It would have been if I could have laid me hands on anythink else. The mean old screw! He paid me little enough for all my work for him.
BROKER	(examining things as he takes them out) Somebody dead, eh?
	(SCROOGE moves U.L. watching.)
CHARWOMAN	Dead as a doornail. (To LAUNDRESS.) And gone to his deserts, I hope.
LAUNDRESS	'Ear, 'ear, the dratted old skinflint.
BROKER	A couple of seals - pencil case - pair of cufflinks - teapot - watch -
	(SCROOGE looks down at his own watch-chain.)
CHARWOMAN	The teapot's silver and the watch is gold.
BROKER	Mrs. Diller, I wish for your sake I could agree with you. but the teapot's plated, and the watch is pinchbeck.
CHARWOMAN	Well, the cheating old varmint! There's a tie-pin there with a pearl in it.
BROKER	This here? (Holds it up.)
CHARWOMAN	That's right.
BROKER	(biting it) Mrs. Diller, there 'ere pearl ain't even been near the smell of an oyster, let alone inside one.
CHARWOMAN	That ain't real, neither?

A CHRISTMAS CAROL

BROKER 'Fraid not, Mrs. Diller.

CHARWOMAN Well, I'm blowed! All his things was just like he was himself - mean, false and shabby. How much for the lot, Joe?

(SCROOGE turns away and leans on desk.)

BROKER Twelve and six, Mrs. Diller, and I'm taking the bread out of the mouths of me children to give it to you.

CHARWOMAN (wheedlingly) Fifteen shillings, Joe.

BROKER Twelve and six, and that's half a crown more than it ought to be.

(He pushes things aside. CHARWOMAN ties them up again.)

(To LAUNDRESS.) Now, what have you got to show me?

(CHARWOMAN breaks up to C. LAUNDRESS rises and comes to top of desk L. and puts big bundle on it.)

Well, you ain't got nothing small by the looks of it? What's inside?

LAUNDRESS (opening it) Blankets, Joe.

(CHARWOMAN moves D.C. to sit on stool, facing U.R.)

BROKER Blankets? His blankets?

LAUNDRESS Whose else, do you think? He won't take cold now for the want of 'em, don't worry.

(SCROOGE moves in to R.C. watching fascinated.)

BROKER (untying bundle) I hope he didn't die of anything catching?

LAUNDRESS No, he didn't. I wouldn't have loitered about to take this blankets off him, if he had. There's a shirt there, too, Joe.

BROKER A shirt, eh?

LAUNDRESS (taking it out) Here you are. The best he had. Not a hole or a darn anywhere. They'd have wasted it if it hadn't been for me.

BROKER (examining shirt) What do you call wasting of it?

LAUNDRESS Putting it on him to be buried in, of course. Somebody was fool enough to do it, but I soon took it off again.

(SCROOGE turns away to desk L. greatly distressed.)

If calico ain't good enough for that purpose, it ain't good enough for anything. And quite as becoming to the body. (Holds up shirt.) He couldn't have looked uglier than he did in this one.

(They all laugh.)

How much for my lot, Joe?

BROKER   Twenty five shillings.

LAUNDRESS   Joe!

BROKER   It's my last word. Take it or leave it.

LAUNDRESS   (disappointed) I'll take it. (Ties up bundle.)

BROKER   Bring 'em into the front shop and I'll pay you the money there.

CHARWOMAN   (rising, moving U.L.) Come on, Mrs. Croucher. We might grind another sixpence out of him.

BROKER   (following them off) I couldn't give you another sixpence, ladies, not if I was to be boiled for not doing it. Thirty-seven and six I'm paying you today and it'll be the ruin of me.

(They have gone out U.L. SCROOGE moves up to C. and stands for a moment with his back to the audience and his hands to his face. The SPIRIT moves to front of desk. SCROOGE turns and kneels before her. Lights fade to candlelight.)

SCROOGE   Spirit, hear me. I am not the man I was. I will not be the man I must have been but for this interlude. Assure me I may yet change these shadows you have shown me by an altered life.

SPIRIT   (moving U.L.) I have nothing more to show you.

SCROOGE   (rising; following for a few steps) I will honour Christmas in my heart and try to keep it all the year. Only tell me I may sponge away the writing on the wall!

SPIRIT   (extending her arm to him, and backing out U.L.) Sleep and remember. Sleep and remember.

A CHRISTMAS CAROL

(She goes out U.L.)

SCROOGE Gone. (He moves down to stool by the fire.) But I will remember. Give me only the chance, and I will live in the past, the present and the future –

(The lights are slowly going down to blackness.)

(Kneeling by stool.) Give me only the chance, good spirit, and I <u>will</u> remember –

(He lays his head on the stool and sleeps. The lights dim down completely until he is illuminated only by the firelight. Hold blackness for a few seconds. Church bells begin to sound offstage, a wild and merry Christmas peal. The lights come slowly up to full. Fade bells as there is the sound of a tuneless voice singing "While Shepherds Watched". The CHARWOMAN enters with a broom. She begins to sweep perfunctorily, still singing. SCROOGE wakes and sees her.)

Goodness gracious!

CHARWOMAN (front of desk R; jumping) Ow! Oh, sir, you did give me a turn! I didn't see you sitting there.

SCROOGE (rising; approaching her) What are you going here?

CHARWOMAN I've come to clean out your office, sir, like I always does.

SCROOGE (hesitating) You – you haven't come to steal my blankets, have you?

CHARWOMAN Steal your – (Indignant.) 'Ere, I'd like you to know, sir, I'm an honest woman I am. (Backs him to C.) Steal your blankets, indeed! What next!

SCROOGE No, no, no, I beg your pardon. It was a mistake – a dream – (Moves L.C.) – at least, I think it was. Er, Mrs. Diller – it <u>is</u> Mrs. Diller, isn't it?

CHARWOMAN That's right, sir.

SCROOGE (moving to her) Then would you have the goodness, Mrs. Diller, to pinch me?

CHARWOMAN Pinch you, sir?

SCROOGE If you would be so kind. (Mystified, she does so. He is overjoyed.) Splendid! I felt that! It's true - I'm alive - I believe I've been given a second chance! Dear me, I'm as light as a feather - I'm as happy as an angel! (He dances MRS. DILLER round.) I'm as merry as a schoolboy - (He releases her and staggers.) I'm as giddy as a drunken man! (He shakes her hand.) A merry Christmas to you, Mrs. Diller, and a happy New Year.

CHARWOMAN Thank you very much, I'm sure.

SCROOGE Mrs. Diller, what day is it?

CHARWOMAN Eh?

SCROOGE The day, Mrs. Diller. What day?

CHARWOMAN It's Christmas Day, of course.

SCROOGE Christmas Day! I haven't missed it, after all! Mrs. Diller, do you know the poulterer's in the next street, on the corner?

CHARWOMAN I should just hope I did.

SCROOGE (patting her shoulder) An intelligent woman - a remarkable woman! Do you know whether they've sold the prize turkey that was hanging up there?

CHARWOMAN What, the one nearly as big as me?

SCROOGE A delightful woman! It's a pleasure to talk to you. (Chucks her under the chin.) Yes, my angel.

CHARWOMAN It's still hanging up there.

SCROOGE Splendid. (Feels in his pocket.) Go and buy it.

CHARWOMAN Buy it!

SCROOGE (handing her coins) Here's the money. (Pushes her in front of him to U.L.) Bring it back here in five minutes and I'll give you half a crown. (He catches her arm as she is about to go off.) Oh, and Mrs. Diller, find a boy, and tell him to run to Mr. Cratchit's and to my niece's house and ask them to have the goodness to step in here.

(MRS. DILLER goes quickly U.L. SCROOGE moves D.C. to fire, rubbing his hands.)

I shall give the turkey to Bob Cratchit. They shall have

A CHRISTMAS CAROL

such a dinner. And to my niece I shall –

(He has picked up the poker and bends to stir the fire into a blaze, when the 1st LADY enters U.L. SCROOGE rises and greets her warmly, putting down poker and moving U.C.)

Ah, come in, madam, come in. I'm delighted to see you. A merry Christmas to you, ma'am.

1st LADY   (moving to him; bewildered)   Thank you, but an elderly woman running from this house requested me to look in and see you. She was afraid you were unwell.

SCROOGE   Unwell? Stuff and nonsense! I was never better in my life.

1st LADY   Then there's nothing I can do for you –

SCROOGE   Ah, but there is, ma'am. (Brings her to R.C.) I was very unwell yesterday, I fear, when you called, and rather unpleasant to you. So in atonement, ma'am, will you accept for your little fund – (Whispers.)

1st LADY   Good gracious! My dear Mr. Scrooge, are you serious?

SCROOGE   If you please, not a farthing less. A great many back payments are included in it, I assure you.

1st LADY   My dear sir, I don't know what to say to such munificence –

SCROOGE   (moving a little D.R.) Then don't say anything at all.

(BOB CRATCHIT, MRS. CRATCHIT, MARTHA and TOM enter U.L. in outdoor things.)

(Crossing to meet them at C.) Ah, my dear Bob Cratchit – and Mrs. Cratchit. (Shakes hands.)

(The CRATCHIT family are astonished. TOM moves down to bottom of L. desk. MARTHA stands in front of the desk.)

BOB   We were just coming from church, sir, when Mrs. Diller met us –

SCROOGE   No apology, Bob. None needed, I assure you. (Crosses him to L. BOB and MRS. CRATCHIT move to 1st LADY, who has moved to bottom of desk R.) So this is Martha and Thomas. (Shakes hands.) How do you do, my dears? Forgive me for keeping you from your dinner for a while, but I hope to season it a little.

A CHRISTMAS CAROL

(BOB during the above, introduces MRS. CRATCHIT to 1st LADY.
MRS. DILLER enters U.L. carrying an enormous brown paper parcel, from which (if possible) the head and legs of a turkey protrude.)

(Moving up C. on MRS. DILLER'S R.)   Ah, Mrs. Diller, back already?   Splendid, splendid!

MRS. DILLER (struggling to feel in pocket)   I got your change here somewhere—

SCROOGE (taking parcel from her)   Keep it, Mrs. Diller, keep it.

(MRS. DILLER, throwing him an astonished glance, makes off quickly U.L.   SCROOGE turns to face MRS CRATCHIT.)

Mrs. Cratchit –   (She turns.)   – in token of the esteem in which I hold your worthy husband –

BOB (incredulously)   Me, sir?

SCROOGE Yes, Bob, you.   (To MRS. CRATCHIT.)   I wish to make you and your family the present of a little poultry.

MRS. C. (moving up to him)   Lord luv a duck, sir!

SCROOGE Not a duck, Mrs. Cratchit.   It's a turkey.

(MRS. CRATCHIT, overwhelmed, takes it and staggers with it to MARTHA and TOM.   They place it on desk L., and examine it while SCROOGE speaks next.)

(Deliberately hardening his voice.)   And as for you, Bob Cratchit, step this way , if you please, sir.

(BOB moves nervously up to SCROOGE'S R.)

You intend to make merry today, I suppose?

BOB Well, I had rather intended to, sir, as far as I could.   It's only once a year, sir.

SCROOGE You shall make merry every day of the year.   I give you notice, Bob –

BOB (horrified)   Notice, sir?

(MRS. CRATCHIT turns, alarmed.)

SCROOGE	Notice that I intend to raise your salary forthwith. (Smiling.) What do you think of that, you dog, you! (Pokes him in the ribs.) What do you think of that?
BOB	Sir - there's nothing I can say but thank you -
SCROOGE	(with a slight tremor in his voice) No, Bob, you can say "A merry Christmas to you, Mr. Scrooge."
BOB	(grasping his hand) A merry Christmas to you, sir, with all my heart!
MRS. C.	(moving to SCROOGE'S L; shaking hands) A merry Christmas, Mr. Scrooge.
	(MARTHA and TOM come up to shake hands. MRS. CRATCHIT crosses to join BOB, and together they move down to discuss the phenomenon with the 1st LADY.)
MARTHA	Merry Christmas, sir.
TOM	Merry Christmas, sir.
SCROOGE	Thank you - thank you all.
BOB	(moving up to him) Sir, our home is only a poor one, but we'd offer you a hearty welcome if you'd come and dine with us.
	(MARTHA and TOM move back to turkey. TOM picks it up.)
MRS. C.	Indeed we would, sir.
SCROOGE	Thank you, Bob. Thank you Mrs. Cratchit, but I hope to be invited somewhere else.
	(SCROOGE'S NIECE enters U.L.)
NIECE	Uncle - (Moves to his L.)
SCROOGE	Fanny - my dear Fanny, so you've come.
NIECE	Uncle, a person said you wished to see me.
SCROOGE	(putting an arm about her) My dear, you were so kind when you called here yesterday as to invite me to share your Christmas with you. Does your invitation still stand?
NIECE	Yes, uncle, indeed it does. Are you coming?

A CHRISTMAS CAROL

SCROOGE Yes, Fanny, my dear, I'm coming.   (He brings her a little D.C.   They stand between the others.)   And I will make it such a merry Christmas – a merrier Christmas than it's been for many a year. A merry Christmas to us all, my dears. God bless us.

BOB (coming to him)   God bless us every one, sir.

(SCROOGE puts his other arm about him.)

SCROOGE Yes, Bob, God bless us – every one.

(MARTHA saying "A merry Christmas, sir" goes out U.L. followed by TOM burdened under the weight of the turkey. The 1st LADY crosses to SCROOGE and shakes him warmly by the hand.)

1st LADY Goodbye, sir, and a merry Christmas to you.

She goes out U.L.   BOB and MRS. CRATCHIT cross SCROOGE and his NIECE to U.L. and exit calling "Merry Christmas".   SCROOGE smiles after them, then moves to hat-stand, and takes down his hat and coat.
The bells begin to peal loudly again off stage.   SCROOGE comes to his niece, offers her his arm, and they walk out happily together.

CURTAIN

PRODUCTION NOTE

The play is equally effective whether presented in curtains or in a box set. In the original award-winning production, the stage was draped with dull brown curtains, with open entrance U.L. and U.R. Furniture need be only of the plainest and shabbiest kind, since Scrooge's meanness is notorious. Ordinary tables constitute the desks, with plain wooden chairs behind them and against the back wall. If possible, the hat stand should be of the old fashioned kind.

Naturally, if the variations of lighting can be managed it will heighten the effect of the play, but it can still be performed with success without these changes, since they are not mentioned in the text. If a wind machine is not available, eerie music can be used instead to precede the entrances of Marley's ghost and the Spirit. This and other sound effects can be recorded on a tape recorder. The dance "Sir Roger de Coverley" should not last too long. About three movements is sufficient, and it may be accompanied either by a piano or a violin.

COSTUMES

All the costumes in the original production were made by the group. The men's clothes were basically old fashioned evening dress suits, with faked high velvet collars at the back, and the buttons changed to brass ones. The trousers were strapped under the shoes, and fancy waistcoats showed a little below the coats. Shirts should be ruffled at front and wrists, and collar points turned up and held in place by high stocks. Fezziwig and Young Scrooge belong to an earlier period and should wear knee breeches and white stockings instead of trousers. If in any doubt, the Dickens illustrations will prove most helpful.

The women's skirts of the period were full, but had not yet attained the circumference of the crinoline. Little short jackets with a basque look most attractive over the full skirts, and it was also a period of muffs and shawls. Fanny, however, and Fezziwig's guests, wear the high-waisted Empire style, as their period is 1801.

Although the cast list includes several male characters an all-women group need not be afraid to tackle the play. The original cast was an all-woman one, and an excellent job they made of it. If wished, several of the characters can be doubled. Scrooge's Niece and Fanny, for example. They are mother and daughter, and a strong family likeness is a natural thing. Mr. Fezziwig and the Pawnbroker may also be played by the same person. Again, the 2nd Lady and Mrs. Fezziwig; while the Laundress and Charwoman can appear earlier as Fezziwig's guests.

The producer should make sure that the pace of the play is maintained. It needs speed and quick cueing if the essential pauses are to be truly effective. The ideal running time is not more than thirty-five minutes, and every endeavour should be made to keep the time within this limit.

Constance Cox